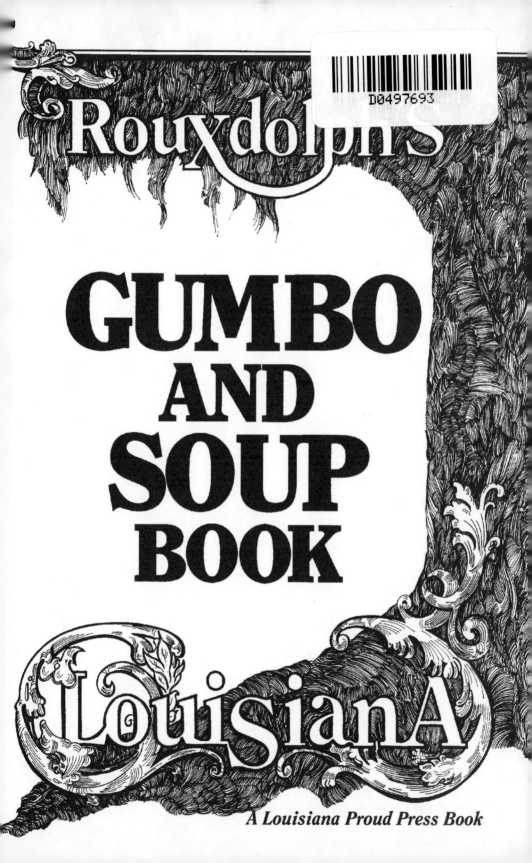

Rouxdolph's

GUMBO AND SOUP BOOK

LouisianA

A Louisiana Proud Press Book

For Information Contact:
Louisiana Proud
6133 Goodwood
Baton Rouge, Louisiana 70806

CONTENTS

Louisiana Cooking has become known world wide for its special flavors. Nothing brings to mind all that is Louisiana Cooking more than the name Gumbo. This famous dish was created in the same manner as the State. The influences of the different cultures gave Louisiana its special blend-its special atmosphere. Gumbo is made from the ingredients and techniques of these varying cultures. It takes a bit from this, a dash from that and pinch of another. They are then placed in a large iron pot and cooked slowly.

When the exiled Acadians settled along the banks of the bayous and lakes they brought with them the basics of French Cooking. What awaited them was a teeming wilderness of wild game, waters laden with various seafoods and the air filled with wild water fowl.

Also in this new world they would discover a new vegetable. This unusual long green fuzzy plant had been brought to the country by African slaves. It was called Kingombo. Today we call it Okra and it is one of the main ingredients of the Louisiana Gumbo.

Traditionally it is said there are but two kinds of Gumbo-Okra and File'. They both act as the thickening agent in the dish. Very rarely do you use both in the same Gumbo. There is, however, a third type, developed for use during the lenten season. It is a vegetable base of greens. Cabbage, lettuce, mustard greens, spinach and the tops of beets and turnips were cooked down and mashed or pureed together to form a thickened base for the gumbo.

The secret of Gumbo is the Roux. This mixture of oil and flour gives the color and flavor so typical of the dish. After the Roux, various ingredients are added as well as the spices and seasonings. The steaming brown mixture is then ladled over bowls of hot fluffy rice and served with French bread.

GUMBO

The most important ingredient in making Gumbo is the Roux. It is the building block, the base for all that comes after it. With a little practice you can produce a Roux exactly the color you want, thereby ensuring a true Louisiana Gumbo.

ROUX

ORIGINAL ROUX

The perfect Roux is a thoroughly mixed colored (from coffee au lait to dark chocolate) thin pudding like paste. The basic ingredients are equal parts of flour and oil. They are combined and stirred together over medium-high to high heat until the desired color is achieved. The cooking process breaks down the flour imparting to the Roux its distinct nutty taste.

The Roux is done when the color you want is achieved. Once it starts to change color it is important to stir frequently, making sure nothing sticks to the bottom of the pot. The closer you come to chocolate brown, the closer you are to a burned Roux. Once the Roux is burned you have to start over. A little practice should solve this problem, however.

After the Roux is the desired color, slowly add hot water, broth, or stock, stirring as you add. It is important that you do not use cold liquid as it may separate the flour and oil. Many cooks stir in a cup of chopped onions to the Roux when the color is right. This will help lower the temperature and prevent burning. They then add the hot liquid of choice.

There are other ways to achieve a Roux, however.

OVEN ROUX

1. Put equal amounts of oil and flour in a pan.
2. Mix thoroughly.
3. Place in 350-400 degree oven.

4. Stir frequently (about every 20 minutes until color is right.
5. Add desired amount to hot water.

   Note: A large amount of Roux can be made at one time by simply increasing the equal amounts of flour and oil. To store additional Roux, let cool and freeze in individual packets.

DRY ROUX

   To make a dry Roux simply follow the steps for Oven Roux leaving out the oil. Place just the desired amount of flour in the pan. When color is right, mix with hot liquid until all the Roux is dissolved.

MARGARINE ROUX

1. Melt 4 sticks margarine in heavy pot.
2. Add 1 cup flour and brown on medium-high to high heat.
3. Stir frequently to avoid burning.
4. When color is right add chopped vegetables to
   reduce cooking temperature.
5. Add hot liquid and mix well.
6. Roux is ready for rest of ingredients.

MICROWAVE ROUX

   Mix equal amounts of flour and oil in microwave safe bowl. A measured pyrex bowl is perfect for this. Simply put in ingredients, mix until creamy paste and place in microwave. Microwave on high for about 4 minutes, stop and stir. Microwave for 2 more minutes. The mixture should be bubbly and starting to turn color. Watch closely as you continue to microwave on high, stopping to stir every 30 to 45 seconds. Remember the darker it gets, the closer it comes to being burned. When the color is as dark as you want, remove from microwave and place in pot. You can add chopped onions and garlic to reduce temperature. Add hot liquid and mix thoroughly. When all the liquid is added, follow the recipe instructions.

FILE'

File' was introduced to the French by the Choctaw Indians. The indians thought the Sassafras tree had special healing powers. They combined the roots and leaves with water to make a healing tonic.

File' is made from the leaves of the Sassafras tree. They were picked fresh and tender, dried and ground into a powder. This finely ground powder was then taken to the markets of New Orleans and sold.

The cooks of New Orleans were quick to discover that File', when added to their Gumbo, produced the same thickening effect as that of okra. It also had added a distinct flavor and coloring to the Gumbo. If heated too long however it will produce a sticky, stringy substance. File' is, therefore, usually added when the heat is turned off or is served in its powdered form at the table. This allows each individual diner to add according to his individual taste.

See pages 24, 33, 46, and 49 for File' Gumbos.

SEASONINGS

Seasonings are the other secret to the Louisiana Gumbo.

Some of the favorite seasonings used are:
Salt
Black Pepper
White Pepper
Cayenne Pepper
(Red Pepper)
Onion Powder
Garlic Powder
Bay leaves
Thyme
Parsley
Wine
Lemon
Tabasco Sauce
File'

While it is true that most Gumbos are on the hot side, seasoning should be a matter of taste. Experiment with the various kinds of seasoning ingredients. Remember, if you are making Gumbo for the first time, start slowly, you can always add more until it is just the way you like it.

STOCKS & BROTHS

Added taste can be achieved in your Soup or Gumbo by making your own stock or broth.

BEEF STOCK
1. Place meat and bone in pot.
2. Fracture bone if possible.
   (This lets out more of the marrow and adds flavor.)
3. Add 2 to 3 quarts water.
4. Cover and simmer about 1 hour.
5. Cut meat from bone.
6. Remove fat and replace meat.
7. Add to Gumbo, Soup or freeze.

CHICKEN STOCK
1. Cut up cleaned chicken and put in pot.
   (Cutting the bones releases more flavor.)
2. Add 2 to 3 quarts water.
3. Cover and simmer about 1 hour.
4. Remove chicken from bones.
5. Remove skin and fat.
6. Replace meat.
7. Add to Gumbo, Soup or freeze.

SEAFOOD STOCK

1. Clean shrimp and save the shells.
2. Place shells in pot and cover with 2 1/2 quarts water.
3. Cover and simmer for 1 hour.
4. Remove shells and strain liquid.
5. Add to Gumbo, Soup or freeze.

RICE

Don't forget the rice!

Rice is almost always served with Gumbo. It is almost always prepared separately, placed in a Gumbo or Soup bowl and the steaming hot Gumbo ladled over it. Some cooks say that the long grain variety is preferred because it won't stick to-gether. They believe that the rice should be fluffy and each individual grain separate.

To make steamed rice:
1. Put 2 cups water in a 2 quart pot.
2. Add 1 cup long grain rice.
3. Add a little salt.
4. Bring to a boil and stir.
5. Cover and reduce to low and cook 20 minutes.
6. Rice is ready when water is gone.

To boil rice:
1. Fill a 4 quart pot with 2 1/2-3 quarts water.
2. Add salt and bring to a boil.
3. Add rice.
   (You can add 2 or 3 cups of rice or desired amount.)
4. Cook 15-16 minutes, stirring frequently.
   (The stirring prevents sticking and makes clean up easier.)
5. Empty in colander and rinse with hot water.
6. Put 2 to 3 inches of water back in pot and bring to boil.
7. Place colander over pot, cover and steam.
8. Fluff with fork occasionally.

Boiling the rice will ensure separated grains if you don't go over the 16 minute cooking mark.

REMEMBER

Start with a Roux.
Do not scorch or burn Roux-Keep stirring during cooking.
Okra thickens Gumbo.
File' left too long will ruin Gumbo.
File' is more often served at the table in its bottled form.
Gumbo without File' can be frozen.
Experiment with seasonings.
Rice should be properly cooked.
Potato salad, French bread, and green salads are
common accompaniments.
Gumbo is better the next day.

GUMBOS

CABBAGE AND SAUSAGE GUMBO
CATFISH GUMBO
CHICKEN AND OYSTER GUMBO
CHICKEN AND SAUSAGE GUMBO
CHICKEN FILE' GUMBO
CHICKEN GUMBO
CHICKEN OKRA GUMBO
CRAB AND OKRA GUMBO
CRAWFISH GUMBO
CREOLE GUMBO
DUCK SAUSAGE GUMBO
FILE' GUMBO
FRENCH MIX GUMBO
GREEN SAUSAGE GUMBO
HEARTY BEEF GUMBO
OKRA GUMBO
SMOKED SAUSAGE AND OKRA GUMBO
SEAFOOD GUMBO
SEAFOOD OKRA GUMBO
SHRIMP GUMBO
SHRIMP AND OYSTER FILE' GUMBO
SQUIRREL GUMBO
TURKEY GUMBO
TURKEY STOCK FILE' GUMBO
WILD GOOSE GUMBO

CABBAGE AND SAUSAGE GUMBO

1 lb. sausage, sliced
1 small cabbage, chopped
1 onion, chopped
1/2 bell pepper, chopped
1 small bunch green onions, chopped
2-3 cloves garlic, chopped
Water
Season to Taste

1. Make a ROUX.
2. Put ROUX in pot, add onion, green onions and garlic.
3. Cook until vegetables are wilted.
4. Add seasonings.
5. Add sausage, 2 qts. water and simmer for 1 hour.
6. Add cabbage and simmer for 25 minutes, covered.
7. Let set for 1 hour before serving.
8. Serve with steaming rice.

CATFISH GUMBO

1 lb. catfish
1 onion, chopped
1 stalk celery, chopped
1/2 bell pepper, chopped
1/2 cup green onion tops, chopped
1 tbsp. parsley, minced
Season to Taste

1. Make a ROUX.
2. Put ROUX in pot and add 2 quarts water.
3. Stir until mixed on medium heat.
4. Add the vegetables and seasonings.
5. Boil, reduce to medium heat and cook for 1 hour.
6. Cut catfish in small pieces and add.
7. Cook until catfish is tender.
8. Serve in bowls over rice.

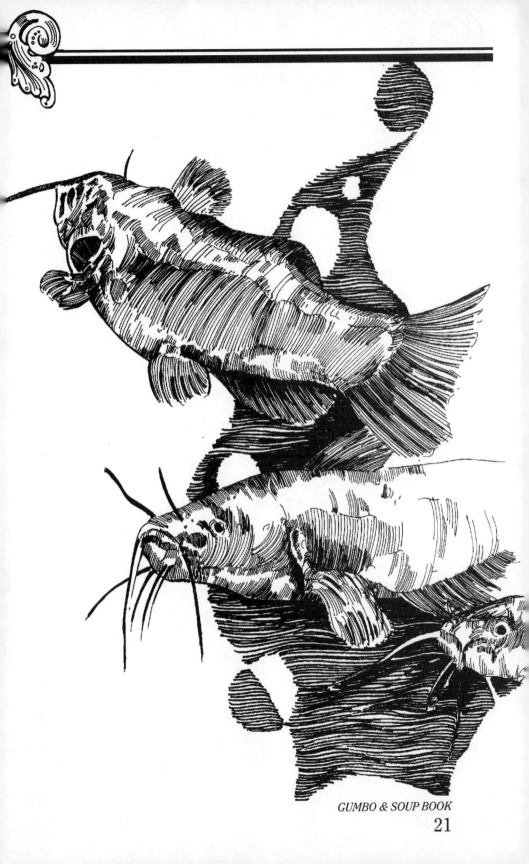

CHICKEN AND OYSTER GUMBO

1 chicken, cut up
1 qt. oysters, save liquid
1 onion, chopped
1 bunch green onions, chopped, including tops
1 clove garlic, chopped
1/2 cup white wine
Water
Season to Taste

1. Make a ROUX.
2. Put ROUX in a pot and add chicken.
3. Slowly add onions and green onions.
4. Cook on high until vegetables are tender.
5. Add 2 qts. water and stir until mixed.
6. Add garlic and seasonings.
7. Bring to a boil then reduce to simmer.
8. Cook until chicken is tender.
9. Add wine, oysters and oyster liquid.
10. Cook until oysters become plump.
11. Serve over fluffy steamed rice.

CHICKEN AND SAUSAGE GUMBO

1 chicken, cut up
2 lbs. sausage, sliced
2 medium onions, chopped
1 medium bell pepper, chopped
1 bunch green onions, chopped
2 tbsp. parsley, chopped
2 cloves garlic, chopped
Water
Season to Taste

1. Make a ROUX.
2. Put cut up chicken in large Gumbo pot.
3. Add 2 qts. water, seasonings and boil for 1/2 hour on high.
4. Add ROUX, sausage, onions, garlic and bell pepper.
5. Simmer for 2 hours or until chicken is tender.
6. Adjust seasonings and water if necessary.
7. Add onion tops and parsley 15 minutes before serving.
8. Serve over steaming mounds of rice.

CHICKEN FILE' GUMBO

1 chicken
2 onions, chopped
2 cloves garlic, chopped
2 stalks celery, chopped
1 bunch green onion tops, chopped
Water
Season to Taste
File'

1. Make a ROUX.
2. Cut up chicken and brown.
3. Add 2 1/2-3 quarts water to ROUX.
4. Add onions, celery, garlic, and seasonings.
5. Bring to boil, then reduce heat and simmer for 1 hour.
6. Remove meat from bones and return to pot.
7. Add green onion tops and simmer 30 minutes longer.
8. Turn off heat and add 1-1 1/2 tbsp. FILE'.
9. Mix well, and serve over bowls of rice.

CHICKEN GUMBO

1 chicken
2 medium onions, chopped
2 stalks celery, chopped
2 cloves garlic, chopped
1/4 cup parsley, chopped
1/4 cup green onion tops, chopped
Water
Season to Taste

1. Make a ROUX.
2. Add vegetables and 3 quarts water.
3. Bring to a boil.
4. Reduce heat to medium and add cut up chicken parts. (Include giblets.)
5. Add seasonings and cook slowly until chicken is done. (Add more water if Gumbo becomes too thick.)
6. Add parsley and green onion tops 15 minutes before serving.
7. Serve in Gumbo bowls or soup plates over rice.

CHICKEN OKRA GUMBO

1 large chicken
2 lbs. okra, sliced thin
1 large tomato, cut in pieces
1 onion, chopped
1 bell pepper, chopped
1 stalk celery, chopped
Cooking oil
Water
Season to Taste

1. Cut chicken in pieces and fry in cooking oil until brown.
2. Remove chicken, leaving enough oil to cover bottom of pot.
3. Add sliced okra and rest of vegetables to pot.
4. Cook on medium until okra stops roping.
   (Stir frequently to prevent sticking.)
5. Add 2 quarts water and seasonings.
6. Add chicken and simmer for 1 1/2 to 2 hours.
7. Serve over steaming hot rice.

CRAB AND OKRA GUMBO

2 lbs. okra, thinly sliced
2 lbs. shrimp, cleaned
1 dozen crabs, boiled and cleaned
2 onions, chopped
1 can tomato sauce
2 cloves garlic, chopped
1 bay leaf
1/4 cup parsley, chopped
Cooking oil
Water
Season to Taste

1. Put shrimp heads in 1 gallon water and boil for 30 minutes.
   (This will become the stock for the Gumbo.)
2. Boil crabs and break them in half.
3. Use enough oil to slowly fry sliced okra until brown.
4. Add tomato sauce and crabs to okra and cook 10 minutes.
5. Add shrimp head stock.
6. Add all ingredients except shrimp and cook slowly for 1 hour.
7. Add shrimp and seasonings and cook slowly for
   2 more hours.
8. Serve hot in bowls of rice.

CRAWFISH GUMBO

3 lbs. crawfish tails, peeled
1 onion, chopped
1 stalk celery, chopped
1/2 bell pepper, chopped
1/2 bunch green onion tops, chopped
1 can Rotel tomatoes, chopped
2 tbsp. parsley, chopped
2-3 cloves garlic, chopped
Water
Season to Taste

1. Make a ROUX.
2. Place ROUX in a pot.
3. Add onions, celery, bell pepper, green onion tops and stir until soft.
4. Add 2 qts. water, Rotel tomatoes and seasonings.
5. Simmer for 1 hour.
6. Add crawfish, garlic, parsley and simmer for 30 minutes.
7. Serve over rice.

CREOLE GUMBO

3 lbs. fresh shrimp, cleaned
1 lb. fresh okra, sliced
2 onions, chopped
1 bunch green onions, chopped
2 tbsp. parsley, chopped
Cooking oil
Water
Season to Taste

1. Make a ROUX.
2. Put ROUX in pot.
3. Smother okra in 3 tbsp. cooking oil.
4. Add onions and green onions and cook until wilted.
5. Add shrimp and cook 5 minutes.
6. Add okra and 2 qts. water and simmer for 1 hour.
7. Add green onions, parsley and seasonings.
8. Simmer for 25 minutes.
9. Serve over hot cooked rice.

DUCK SAUSAGE GUMBO

2-3 ducks
1 lb. smoked sausage
1 cup onion, chopped
1 cup bell pepper, chopped
1 cup celery, chopped
2 tbsp. green onion tops, chopped
Water
Season to Taste

1. Make a ROUX.
2. Put ROUX in pot and add onion, bell pepper, and celery.
3. Slowly add 3-4 quarts water, stirring constantly.
4. Cut up and brown ducks.
5. Add ducks and seasonings.
6. Simmer for 1 1/2-2 hours.
7. Add sausage and simmer for 1 more hour.
8. Add onion tops the last 15 minutes.
9. Adjust seasoning.
10. Serve over rice.

FILE' GUMBO

1 chicken
1 lb. sausage
2 dozen oysters (retain liquid)
2 onions, chopped
2 cloves garlic, chopped
1/2 bunch green onion tops, chopped
2 bay leaves
Water
Season to Taste
File'

1. Make a ROUX.
2. Cut up chicken into pieces.
3. Season and lightly brown cut up chicken pieces.
4. Add chicken, sausage, and onions to ROUX.
5. Add 1 1/2-2 quarts water and bring to a boil.
6. Add bay leaves, garlic and seasonings.
7. Reduce heat and simmer for 1 hour.
8. Remove bones from chicken and return meat to pot.
9. Simmer for 1 more hour.
10. Add oysters and oyster liquid.
11. Cook 3-5 minutes until oysters start to curl.
12. Turn off heat and add 1-2 tbsp. FILE'.
13. Slowly mix FILE' with gumbo.
14. Serve over rice.

FRENCH MIX GUMBO

2 lbs. fresh fish
1 lb. shrimp, cleaned
1 lb. crab meat
2 onions, chopped
2 stalks celery, chopped
1 bunch green onion tops, chopped
1/2 bell pepper, chopped
2 cloves garlic, chopped
2 cups Burgundy wine
2 tbsp. parsley, chopped
Water
Season to Taste

1. Make a ROUX
2. Put ROUX in pot, add onions, celery, bell pepper and garlic.
3. Heat on medium until vegetables wilt.
4. Add 2 quarts water.
5. Add seasonings and cook for 1 hour on medium.
6. Add fish and cook until tender.
7. Add shrimp, crab meat and wine and cook for 15 minutes.
8. Add parsley and cook 5 more minutes.
9. Serve over rice.

GREEN SAUSAGE GUMBO

1 lb. sausage
1 small head of cabbage
1 small bunch of spinach or mustard
1 stalk celery
2 onions
1 cup parsley
2 cloves garlic
Water
Season to Taste

1. Make a ROUX.
2. Put all vegetables in blender.
3. Add 2 quarts water to ROUX and bring to boil.
4. Reduce heat to medium and add blended vegetables.
5. Add sausage and seasonings.
6. Cook for 1 1/2 to 2 hours.
7. Serve over rice.

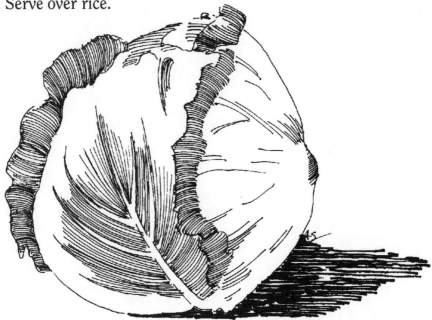

HEARTY BEEF GUMBO

1 lb. stew meat, cubed
1 lb. fresh okra, sliced
1 can beef broth
2 onions, chopped
1 bell pepper, chopped
3-4 cloves garlic, chopped
1/2 cup green onion tops, chopped
1 cup Burgundy wine
Cooking oil
Water
Season to Taste

1. Brown meat in 3 tbsp. cooking oil.
2. Remove meat and add 1 tbsp. cooking oil to pot.
3. Add okra and cook until done.
   (Okra is done when it stops roping.)
4. Make a ROUX.
5. Add meat, vegetables, garlic and 2 qts. water to ROUX.
6. Add seasonings, wine, beef broth and onion tops.
7. Simmer until meat is tender, about 1 hour.
8. Serve with steamed rice.

OKRA GUMBO

2 lbs. okra, sliced thin
1 onion, chopped
1 bell pepper, chopped
1 stalk celery, chopped
2 cloves garlic, chopped
1/2 can tomato paste
Cooking oil
Water
Season to Taste

1. Cover bottom of heavy pot with cooking oil and heat until hot.
2. Reduce heat to medium and add thinly sliced okra. (Stir constantly to prevent sticking.)
3. Add onion, bell pepper, and celery. (Okra is done when brown and the sticky substance is gone.)
4. Add 2 quarts water and tomato paste.
5. Add seasonings, cover and simmer for 1 hour.
6. Serve over rice.

SMOKED SAUSAGE AND OKRA GUMBO

1 lb. smoked sausage or tasso
2 lbs. okra
1 onion, chopped
1 bell pepper, chopped
1 can tomatoes
2 cloves garlic, chopped
Cooking oil
Water
Season to Taste

1. Cut okra into thin slices
2. Cover bottom of pot with cooking oil and heat.
3. Reduce heat to medium and add okra and cover pot.
   (Stir often to prevent sticking.)
4. When okra is brown, add onion, bell pepper and garlic.
5. Add tomatoes and 2 quarts water.
6. Cut sausage or tasso in small pieces and add.
7. Add seasoning.
   (Adjust if sausage or tasso is already seasoned.)
8. Cook on medium for 1 1/2-2 hours.
9. Adjust seasoning and stir frequently.
   (Add more water if Gumbo becomes too thick.)
10. Serve in Gumbo bowls over rice.

SEAFOOD GUMBO

1 doz. whole crabs
1 lb. shrimp, cleaned
1 qt. oysters
2 onions, chopped
4 green onions, chopped
2 stalks celery, chopped
1 bell pepper, chopped
2 tbsp. parsley
2 cloves garlic, chopped
Water
Season to Taste

1. Make a ROUX.
2. Put ROUX in pot and add onions, celery,
   bell pepper and garlic.
3. Add 3 qts. water, bring to boil and stir well.
4. Reduce heat to medium and add seasonings.
5. Add crabs and cook for 1 hour.
6. Add shrimp and oyster liquid, parsley and green onions.
7. Cook until shrimp are done.
8. 15 minutes before serving, add oysters.
9. Serve over steamed rice.

SEAFOOD OKRA GUMBO

2 lbs. okra, sliced
2 lbs. shrimp
1 qt. oysters
2 lbs. crab meat
2 medium onions, chopped
1 green pepper, chopped
2 cans whole tomatoes, chopped
2 cloves garlic, chopped
1 bay leaf
Cooking oil
Water
Season to Taste

1. Cook shrimp in 2 qts. water for about 30 minutes.
2. Shell shrimp and save the broth.
3. Cover bottom of large pot with oil .
4. Add okra, onions, green peppers and garlic.
5. Cook on low heat stirring frequently until
   vegetables are done.
   (Vegetables are done when okra stops roping)
6. Add tomatoes and stir to blend.
7. Add shrimp broth, oyster liquid, bay leaf and seasonings.
8. Add shrimp and crab meat and simmer 45 minutes.
9. Add oysters and cook until done, about 10 or 15 minutes.
10. Serve in Gumbo or soup bowls over rice.

SHRIMP GUMBO

2 lbs. shrimp, peeled
1 onion, chopped
1/2 cup green onion tops, chopped
1 tbsp. parsley, chopped
Water
Season to Taste

1. Make a ROUX
2. Put ROUX and onion in large pot.
3. Heat until onion wilts.
4. Add 2 quarts water.
5. Add seasonings.
6. Boil, reduce to medium and cook for an hour.
7. Stir frequently.
8. Add shrimp and cook for 20 minutes.
9. Add onion tops and parsley and cook for 10 minutes.
10. Serve over cooked rice.

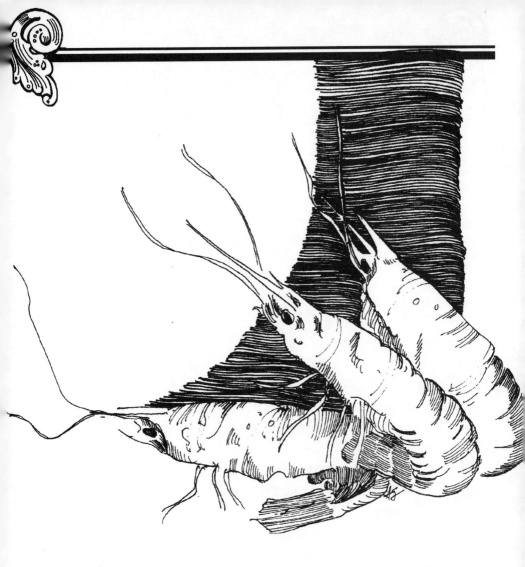

SHRIMP AND OYSTER FILE' GUMBO

2 lbs. shrimp
2 dozen oysters (retain liquid)
2 onions, chopped
2 garlic cloves, chopped
1/2 bunch of green onion tops, chopped
Dry red wine
Water
Season to Taste
File'

1. Make a ROUX.
2. Add 1 1/2 quarts seafood stock to ROUX.
   (Use shrimp shells to make the seafood stock.)
3. Add onions, garlic, and seasonings.
4. Simmer for 1 hour.
5. Add cleaned and peeled shrimp.
6. Add 1 cup dry red wine and chopped onion tops.
7. Cook for 15 minutes.
8. Add oysters and oyster liqiud.
9. Cook 3-5 minutes until oysters start to curl.
10. Turn off heat and add 1-1 1/2 tbsp. FILE'
11. Mix well and let set for 10 minutes.
12. Serve over rice.

SQUIRREL GUMBO

4-6 squirrels
1 lb. smoked sausage, sliced
1 large onion, chopped
2 tbsp. green onion tops, chopped
2 tbsp. fresh parsley, chopped
Water
Season to Taste

1. Make a ROUX.
2. Put ROUX in pot and add 2 quarts water.
3. Put on medium heat and stir until blended.
4. Add onions, cut up squirrel, sausage and seasonings.
5. Cook until meat is tender.
   (About 1 hour.)
6. Add onion tops and parsley and cook 10-15 minutes more.
7. Serve in Gumbo bowls over rice.

TURKEY GUMBO

1 turkey carcass
1 lb. sausage, sliced
2 onions, chopped
1 bell pepper, chopped
2 stalks celery, chopped
3 cloves garlic, chopped
1 large tomato, chopped
Water
Season to Taste

1. Put turkey carcass and seasonings in pot and cover with 2 qts. water .
2. Boil 1 1/2 to 2 hours.
3. Strain, remove bones and save broth and meat.
4. Make a ROUX.
5. Put ROUX in pot, add sausage and vegetables.
6. Add broth and turkey meat and bring to a boil.
7. Reduce heat, add tomatoes, seasonings and simmer 1 hour.
8. Adjust seasonings and water if necessary.
9. Serve over rice.

TURKEY STOCK FILE' GUMBO

1 turkey carcass
1 lb. shrimp, cleaned
1/2 lb. sausage
2 onions, chopped
2 stalks celery, chopped
2 cloves garlic, chopped
1 small bell pepper, chopped
1 bay leaf
Water
Season to Taste
File'

1. Place carcass in large pot and add 2 quarts water.
2. Boil for 1 hour, remove bones and return meat to pot.
3. Make a ROUX and add to turkey stock.
4. Add onions, celery, bell pepper, garlic and bay leaf.
5. Add sausage and seasonings and simmer for 30 minutes.
6. Add cleaned shrimp and simmer for 15-20 minutes.
7. Turn off heat and add 1-1 1/2 t bsp. FILE'.
8. Mix well and let stand 15 minutes.
9. Serve over rice.

WILD GOOSE GUMBO

1 goose
1 onion, chopped
1 stalk celery, chopped
1 bell pepper, chopped
1 bunch green onions, chopped
Water
Season to Taste

1. Rub seasonings inside and outside of goose.
2. Stuff goose with onion, celery, and bell pepper.
3. Bake at 350 degrees until tender.
4. Make a ROUX.
5. Add 4 quarts water to ROUX and bring to boil.
6. Remove vegetables from goose and cut up into pieces.
7. Add vegetables and goose to ROUX mixture.
8. Adjust seasoning and simmer for one hour.
9. Add chopped green onions, including tops, 15 minutes before serving over rice.

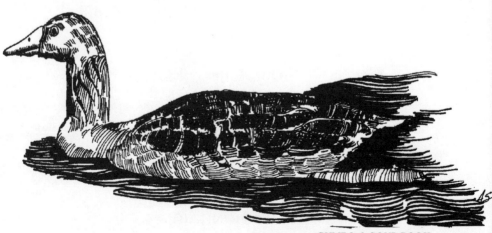

ALLIGATOR SOUP
ARTICHOKE SOUP
BLACK BEAN SOUP
BROCCOLI AND CHEESE SOUP
BROCCOLI CREAM SOUP
CHEEZY SQUASH SOUP
CORN AND SHRIMP SOUP
CORN CRAB SOUP
CORN SOUP
CRAB SOUP
CREAM OF TOMATO SOUP
CREAMY FRESH MUSHROOM SOUP
CURRY POTATO SOUP
EILEEN'S CHUNKY SPLIT PEA SOUP
FOWL WEATHER SOUP
FRENCH ONION SOUP
FRONT PORCH SOUP
HARE SOUP
HOBO SOUP
LETTUCE SOUP
LOUISIANA LENTIL SOUP
MUSHROOM SOUP
OKRA SOUP
ONION SOUP
OYSTER AND ARTICHOKE SOUP
OYSTER SOUP
POTATO SOUP
QUICK RED BEAN SOUP
RED BEAN SOUP
ROUGE SOUP
SAUERKRAUT SOUP
SHRIMP ONION SOUP
TURTLE SOUP
VEGETABLE SOUP
WORKING MOM SOUP

SOUPS

ALLIGATOR SOUP

2 lbs. alligator meat, cubed
2 onions, chopped
2 stalks celery, chopped
2-3 cloves garlic, chopped
1 can Rotel tomatoes, chopped
Beef broth
Sherry wine
2 bay leaves
Parsley
Flour
Butter
Water
Season to Taste

1. Brown alligator meat in 1 stick butter.
2. Saute onions, celery and garlic in 2 tbsp. butter.
3. Mix sauteed vegetables and alligator meat.
4. Add 1/2 cup flour and mix well.
5. Add 2 qts. beef broth, bay leaves and tomatoes.
6. Add seasonings and simmer for 1-1/2 to 2 hours.
7. Add 2 tbsp. parsley and 1 cup sherry wine.
8. Simmer for 10-15 minutes.

ARTICHOKE SOUP

2 cans artichoke hearts, chopped
1 bunch green onions, chopped
1 stalk celery, chopped
2 cloves garlic, chopped
1 qt. chicken broth
1 cup Half and Half
Butter
Season to Taste

1. Saute green onions, celery and garlic in 2 tbsp. butter.
2. Add seasonings and broth.
3. Simmer 15-20 minutes.
4. Add artichoke hearts and simmer 10 minutes.
5. Add Half and Half and mix well.
6. Simmer 5-10 minutes and serve.

BLACK BEAN SOUP

1 lb. black beans
1 lb. smoked sausage
2 onions, chopped
1 bell pepper, chopped
1 stalk celery, chopped
2 cloves garlic, chopped
1 can Rotel tomatoes, chopped
Burgundy wine
Butter
Water
Season to Taste

1. Cover beans with water and soak overnight.
2. Drain beans and add 2 qts. water.
3. Add sausage and simmer for 1-1 1/2 hours.
4. Saute vegetables in 2 tbsp. butter.
5. Add sauteed vegetables, tomatoes and seasonings.
6. Simmer for 2 hours.
7. Put mixture through blender.
8. Add wine and re-heat for 10 minutes.
9. Serve hot.

BROCCOLI AND CHEESE SOUP

2 boxes chopped broccoli
3 cans chicken broth
1 roll garlic cheese
1 roll jalapeno cheese
1 small bunch green onions, chopped
Butter
Flour
Milk
Season to Taste

1. Cook broccoli according to package and drain.
2. Saute green onions in 2 tbsp. butter.
3. Add 2 tbsp. flour and cook until smooth.
4. Slowly add 2 cups milk.
5. Cut rolls of cheese into chunks and add.
6. Stir until melted.
7. Add broccoli and chicken broth.
8. Simmer 10-15 minutes and serve.

BROCCOLI CREAM SOUP

2 lbs. fresh broccoli
2 qts. chicken broth
1 large onion, chopped
1 small bunch green onions, chopped
1 stalk celery, chopped
2 cups Half and Half
Butter
Flour
Season to Taste

1. Cut 1 lb. of broccoli into stems and flowers and put in pot.
2. Add 1 qt. chicken broth and boil for 30 minutes.
3. Saute onions, celery, and green onions in 2 or 3 tbsp. of butter.
4. Strain the broccoli and chicken broth into another pot.
5. Add the other quart of chicken broth.
6. Add the sauteed vegetables and 2 tbsp. of flour.
7. Cook for 5 minutes, stirring frequently.
8. Cut 1 lb. broccoli into pieces and add to soup.
9. Add seasonings.
10. Slowly blend in 2 cups Half and Half.
11. Gently heat for 10 minutes and serve.

CHEEZY SQUASH SOUP

2 medium zucchini, sliced thin
2 medium yellow squash, sliced thin
2 onions, chopped thin
2 cups chicken stock
1 cup Half and Half
6 oz. Colby cheese, grated
Butter
Flour
Season to Taste

1. Saute zucchini, squash, and onions in 1 stick butter.
2. When limp add 2 tbsp. flour.
3. Simmer 5 minutes, mixing thoroughly.
4. Add chicken stock and seasonings.
5. Simmer 15 minutes stirring constantly.
6. Add cheese and stir.
7. When melted, blend in Half and Half.
8. Heat, but do not boil.
9. Serve hot.

CORN AND SHRIMP SOUP

2 lbs. shrimp, peeled
8 ears fresh corn
2 onions, chopped
2 fresh tomatoes, chopped
Flour
Butter
Water
Season to Taste

1. Saute onions in 1 tbsp. flour and 1 tbsp. butter.
2. Cut corn from the cob with knife.
3. Add shrimp, corn, tomatoes and onions to pot.
4. Add seasonings and 2 qts. water.
5. Simmer for 1-1/2 to 2 hours.

CORN CRAB SOUP

1 lb. crab meat
2 onions, chopped
1 bunch green onions, chopped
3 stalks celery, chopped
1 can corn
2 pints Half and Half
Butter
Season to Taste

1. Saute onions, green onions and celery in 1 stick of butter.
   (Until onions are clear, not brown.)
2. Add corn and simmer for 10 minutes.
3. Slowly add Half and Half and mix well.
4. Add seasonings.
5. Add crab meat.
6. Simmer 10 minutes and serve.

CORN SOUP

10 ears of corn
1 lb. pickle meat
1 can tomato sauce
1/2 cup ketchup
6 potatoes, cut into pieces
1 cup green lima beans
1 onion, chopped
1/2 bell pepper, chopped
2 tbsp. cooking oil
Water
Season to Taste

1. Cut corn off cob, scraping with knife.
2. Smother corn, meat, onion and bell pepper for 30 minutes.
3. Add tomato sauce and ketchup and cook for 15 minutes.
4. Add 2 qts. water and boil for 30 minutes.
5. Add lima beans and potatoes.
6. Add seasonings and 1 qt. water.
7. Boil until potatoes are done.
   (If too thick add 2 cups of water and bring to a boil.)

CRAB SOUP

1 lb. crab meat
1 onion, chopped
1 can whole tomatoes, chopped
2 cloves garlic, chopped
2 lemons
Butter
Water
Season to Taste

1. Saute onions and garlic in 1 tbsp butter.
2. Add 1 1/2 qts. water.
3. Bring to a boil.
4. Reduce to simmer.
5. Add seasonings and tomatoes and simmer for 30 minutes.
6. Add crab meat and simmer 15 minutes.
7. Add the juice from 2 lemons and serve hot.

CREAM OF TOMATO SOUP

1 bunch green onions with tops, chopped
1 can beef broth
2 cans whole tomatoes
1 cup Half and Half
Sugar
Butter
Flour
Season to Taste

1. Saute onions in 2 tbsp. butter until limp.
2. Add 2 tbsp. flour and seasonings, blending well.
3. Add sugar, beef broth, and Half and Half.
4. Heat slowly, blending constantly until smooth and creamy
5. Put tomatoes and juice in blender and puree.
6. Add tomato puree to pot and simmer for 15-20 minutes.
7. Do not Boil.

CREAMY FRESH MUSHROOM SOUP

1 lb. fresh mushrooms
10 cups chicken broth
1 qt. Half and Half
Butter
Flour
Season to Taste

1. Saute mushrooms in 2 sticks butter.
2. When soft, add 1/3 cup flour and blend until smooth.
   (Do not brown flour and mushrooms.)
3. When smooth add chicken broth.
4. Simmer for 15-20 minutes.
5. Add seasonings.
6. Fold in Half and Half.
7. Simmer 5 minutes and serve.

CURRY POTATO SOUP

2 white potatoes, chopped
1 onion, chopped
1 stalk celery with leaves, chopped
2 cups milk
2 cans chicken broth
2 tbsp. curry powder
Season to Taste

1. Mix all ingredients together.
2. Add seasonings.
3. Add curry powder
4. Heat until potatoes are tender.
5. Serve in soup bowls.

EILEEN'S CHUNKY SPLIT PEA SOUP

1 lb. green split peas
6 fresh ham hocks or 1 lb. pickle meat
3 large onions, chopped
4 carrots, chopped
3 stalks celery, chopped
3 garlic cloves, chopped
Water
Season to Taste

1. Wash and sort peas.
2. Place all ingredients in large pot.
3. Add 6 pints of water to start.
4. Boil 2-2 1/2 hours, until peas are a thick soup consistency. (Carrots should still be recognizable.)
5. Add milk or water to achieve desired consistency.
6. Serve in large bowl with hock in soup or on side.
7. Great with crusty garlic French bread.
   NOTE: If using pickle meat, add it during last 45 minutes of cooking.

FOWL WEATHER SOUP

1 chicken
1 link pork sausage, sliced
2 onions, chopped
2 stalks celery, chopped
2 small carrots, sliced
2 cloves garlic, chopped
1 bell pepper, chopped
Water
Season to Taste

1. Cut up chicken and put in pot.
2. Add 2 quarts water and boil for 1 hour.
3. Remove chicken from bones and return to pot.
4. Add sliced sausage, onions, celery, carrots, and bell pepper.
5. Add garlic and seasonings.
6. Simmer for 3/4-1 hour.

FRENCH ONION SOUP

18-20 onions, sliced
2 qts. beef stock
2-3 cloves garlic, chopped
1 bay leaf
Butter
French bread, toasted and sliced
Parmesan cheese
Season to Taste

1. Saute onions in 1 stick butter until brown.
2. Add beef stock, bay leaf, and other seasonings.
3. Simmer 1 hour.
4. Remove bay leaf and ladle into soup bowls.
5. Float French bread on each serving.
6. Sprinkle Parmesan cheese on French bread and serve.

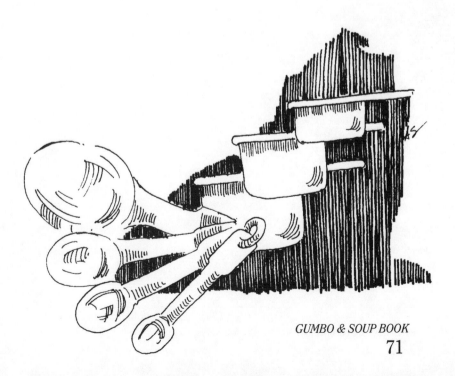

FRONT PORCH SOUP

2 boxes frozen spinach, chopped
1 lb. smoked sausage, sliced
1 lb. pickle meat, cut in chunks
1 lb. navy beans
4 white potatoes, cut in chunks
2-3 cloves garlic, chopped
Water
Season to Taste

1. Soak beans overnight.
2. Add spinach, potatoes, pickle meat and sausage.
3. Add 3 qts. water and seasonings.
4. Simmer 3 hours.

HARE SOUP

2-3 lbs. rabbit
2 onions, chopped
1 stalk celery, chopped
1/2 bell pepper, chopped
2 cloves garlic, chopped
Red wine
Water
Season to Taste

1. Skin and wash rabbit meat.
2. Cut meat in pieces.
3. Put meat in pot and add 2 quarts water.
4. Add vegetables and seasonings.
5. Simmer for 2 hours or until meat is tender.
6. Add 1/2 cup wine 15 minutes before serving.
7. Serve over hot rice.

HOBO SOUP

2 lbs. stew meat
1 lb. smoked sausage
2 onions, chopped
1 bell pepper, chopped
3 stalks celery, chopped
4-6 carrots, sliced
2 large potatoes, chopped
1 can Rotel tomatoes
2 cans mixed vegetables
1 large can tomato sauce
2 tbsp. parsley
Water
Season to Taste

1. Put 4 qts. water, stew meat and sausage into large pot.
2. Boil for 30 minutes.
3. Add all other ingredients and seasonings.
4. Simmer for 1-1 1/2 hours stirring frequently.
5. Serve when meat is tender.

LETTUCE SOUP

1 head lettuce, chopped
2 green onions, chopped
3 cans chicken broth
1/2 cup milk
Butter
Water
Season to Taste

1. Put lettuce in pot.
2. Add enough water, about 1 cup, and cook until tender.
3. Saute onions in 2 tbsp. butter and add to pot.
4. Add chicken broth, milk and seasonings.
5. Bring to a boil then reduce heat to simmer.
6. Simmer for about 15 minutes.
7. Serve with croutons.

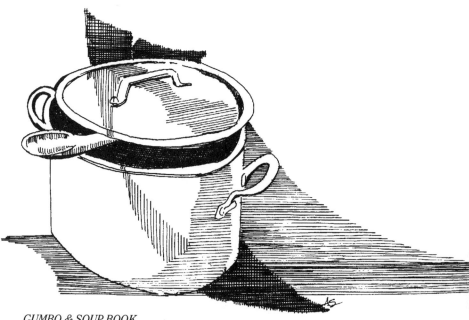

LOUISIANA LENTIL SOUP

1 lb. lentil beans, dried
1 lb. smoked sausage, sliced
1 onion, chopped
1/2 bell pepper, chopped
1 stalk celery, chopped
Cooking oil
Flour
Water
Season to Taste

1. Soak lentils overnight.
2. Saute onions, bell pepper and celery in 2 tbsp. oil and flour.
3. Place the drained lentils in a large pot.
4. Add 2 1/2 qts. water, sausage and sauteed vegetables.
5. Add seasonings.
6. Simmer for 2 1/2 to 3 hours.

MUSHROOM SOUP

1 1/2 lbs. fresh mushrooms
6 cans beef broth
1 onion, chopped fine
1 bunch green onion tops, chopped
2 cloves garlic, chopped
Butter
Flour
Season to Taste

1. Wash and slice mushrooms.
2. Add mushrooms and beef broth to pot.
3. Simmer 30 minutes.
4. Saute onion, garlic, and onion tops in 2 tbsp. of butter.
5. Add 2 tbsp. flour to saute and mix throughly.
6. Add sauteed vegetables to mushrooms and broth.
7. Add seasonings.
8. When mixed and throughly heated, Serve.

OKRA SOUP

2 lbs. lean stew meat, cubed
2 lbs. fresh okra, sliced
2 onions, chopped
1 bell pepper, chopped
1 bunch green onions, chopped
2 cloves garlic, chopped
Butter
Water
Season to Taste

1. Brown beef in 1 stick butter.
2. Add onion, bell pepper, green onions and garlic.
3. Cook until vegetables wilt.
4. Add 3 qts. water.
5. Add seasonings and simmer for 1 hour.
6. Add okra and simmer for 3 hours.

ONION SOUP

4-5 onions, sliced
4 cans beef broth
Butter
Toasted French bread, sliced
Parmesan cheese, grated
Water
Flour
Season to Taste

1. Saute onions in 4 tbsp. butter.
2. Add beef broth and simmer for 45 minutes.
3. Brown 2 tbsp. butter and 2 tbsp. flour.
4. Add 1 qt. water to browned flour.
5. Add two mixtures together and simmer for 30 minutes.
6. Ladle soup into soup bowls.
7. Float sliced French bread and sprinkle with
   Parmesan cheese.

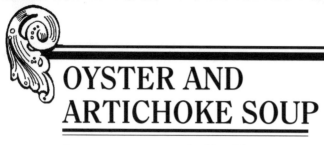

OYSTER AND ARTICHOKE SOUP

2 qts. oysters, retain liquid
2 cans artichokes, retain liquid
1 can chicken broth
1 onion, chopped
2 stalks celery, chopped
2 cloves garlic, chopped
Butter
Flour
Water
Season to Taste

1. Saute onions, celery and garlic in 2 tbsp. butter.
2. Add 2 tbsp. flour to sauteed vegetables and cook for 5 minutes.
3. Add 2 qts. water and seasonings.
4. Add chicken broth, artichokes and liquid.
5. Heat for 10 minutes.
6. Add oysters and liquid and heat 10-15 minutes.
7. Serve when oysters are plump.

OYSTER SOUP

1 qt. oysters, retain liquid
1 bunch green onions, chopped
1 stalk celery, chopped
2 cloves garlic, chopped
Parsley
1 bay leaf
Flour
Butter
Milk
Season to Taste

1. Saute onions, garlic and celery in 1/2 stick butter.
2. Saute for 3 minutes or until onions are limp.
3. Add flour and cook for 3 minutes.
4. Combine oyster liquid and milk to make 1 1/2 qts.
5. Add oyster liquid/milk, 2 tbsp. parsley and bay leaf.
6. Add seasonings and bring to a boil.
7. Simmer for 15-20 minutes.
8. Add oysters and simmer 5-10 minutes or until plump.

POTATO SOUP

6 white potatoes, quartered
1 can Golden Mushroom Soup
1 lb. ham, diced
1 can carrots
1 can green peas
Milk
Butter
Parsley
Water
Season to taste

1. Boil potatoes.
2. Puree carrots and peas in a blender.
3. Pour off all but 2 cups water from potatoes.
4. Mash potatoes in remaining water.
5. Add 1 qt. of milk.
6. Add Golden Mushroom Soup and 1 can of water.
7. Add the carrots, peas, 1 stick butter and parsley.
8. Add ham and seasonings.
9. Simmer for 15-20 minutes, then serve.

QUICK RED BEAN SOUP

1 can red kidney beans
1 lb. ham, chopped fine
1 onion, chopped
1/2 bell pepper, chopped
1 stalk celery, chopped
2 cloves garlic, chopped
1 bay leaf
Butter
Burgundy wine
Water
Season to Taste

1. Saute onion, garlic, bell pepper and celery in 2 tbsp. butter.
2. Place sauteed vegetables into a pot with 1 qt. water.
3. Add beans and bay leaf and simmer for 1 hour.
4. Stir frequently mashing beans in the pot.
5. Add ham, seasonings and 1/2 cup wine.
6. Mix well and heat for 5 minutes and serve.

RED BEAN SOUP

1 lb. red beans
3 smoked ham hocks
3 onions, chopped
1 bell pepper, chopped
2 stalks celery, chopped
3 cloves garlic, chopped
1 bay leaf
2 tbsp. parsley, chopped
Water
Season to Taste

1. Put 4 qts. water in large pot.
2. Add beans, onions, bell pepper, garlic, celery, bay leaf and parsley.
3. Add ham hocks and seasonings.
4. Bring to a boil.
5. Simmer for 3 hours, stirring frequently.
6. Remove ham hocks.
7. Force all the mixture through a strainer and back into a pot.
8. Cut meat into bite size pieces.
   (If soup becomes too thick add more water.)
9. Heat and serve.

ROUGE SOUP

1 bunch beets
1 1/2 to 2 lbs. ham, chunked
2 onions, chopped
2 potatoes, chunked
2 stalks celery, chopped
2 carrots, sliced
1 can beef broth
1 can whole tomatoes, chopped
2-3 cloves garlic, chopped
2 bay leaves
Water
Season to Taste

1. Put 2 qts. water in pot.
2. Add ham chunks, beets, bay leaves and garlic.
3. Boil until beets are tender.
4. Remove beets and slice.
5. Return beets to soup pot.
6. Add onions, potatoes, celery, tomatoes and beef broth.
7. Add seasonings.
8. Simmer for 45 minutes to 1 hour.
9. Serve when vegetables are done.

SAUERKRAUT SOUP

1 can sauerkraut, chopped
1 lb. smoked sausage, sliced
2 onions, chopped
1 tbsp. flour
2 tbsp. butter
Water
Season to Taste

1. Put sauerkraut and juice into pot and simmer.
2. Saute onions in 2 tbsp. butter and add to pot.
3. Add sausage and 1 1/2 cans of water.
4. Add seasonings.
5. Add flour and mix well.
6. Simmer about 30 minutes.
7. Serve hot.

SHRIMP ONION SOUP

2 lbs. shrimp, peeled
6 large onions, sliced
1 small bunch green onions with tops, chopped
2 cloves garlic, chopped
2 quarts chicken broth
Flour
Butter
Season to Taste

1. Saute onions and green onions in 2 sticks of butter.
2. Add 4 tbsp. flour and mix well.
3. Add chicken broth, stir, and cook 15 minutes on medium.
4. Add shrimp and seasonings.
5. Serve when shrimp are done.

TURTLE SOUP

2 lbs. turtle meat
3 onions, chopped
1 bell pepper, chopped
3 stalks celery, chopped
1 can Rotel tomatoes
2 cans tomato sauce
1 small bunch green onions, chopped
Parsley
Bay leaf
Cooking oil
Sherry wine
Season to Taste

1. Cube turtle meat and fry in oil until brown.
2. Remove meat from pot and save.
3. Saute onions, bell pepper and celery in 2 tbsp cooking oil.
4. Add 2 qts. water, sauteed vegetables and turtle meat.
5. Simmer for 30 minutes.
6. Add seasonings, tomatoes, bay leaf and tomato sauce.
7. Simmer for 1 hour.
8. Add 1 cup wine, green onions and 2 tbsp. parsley.
9. Simmer for 20-30 minutes or until meat is tender.

VEGETABLE SOUP

2 lbs. stew meat
2 onions, chopped
3 carrots, sliced
3 tomatoes, chopped
2 potatoes, diced
1 can green lima beans
1 can corn
2 tbsp. parsley
2 cloves garlic, chopped
Water
Season to Taste

1. In large soup pot brown stew meat.
2. Add 4 qts. water and seasonings.
3. Simmer for 1 1/2 to 2 hours.
4. Add all other ingredients and simmer for 1 hour.

WORKING MOM SOUP

1 lb. stew meat, cut into bite size pieces
1 small can carrots
1 large can corn
1 large can green beans
1 small can green lima beans
1 can whole tomatoes
1 small can tomato sauce
Cooking oil
Season to Taste

1. Saute meat in 2 tbsp. cooking oil in large pot.
2. Add all vegetables and their juices.
3. Add tomato sauce.
4. Add seasonings.
5. Simmer until meat is tender.

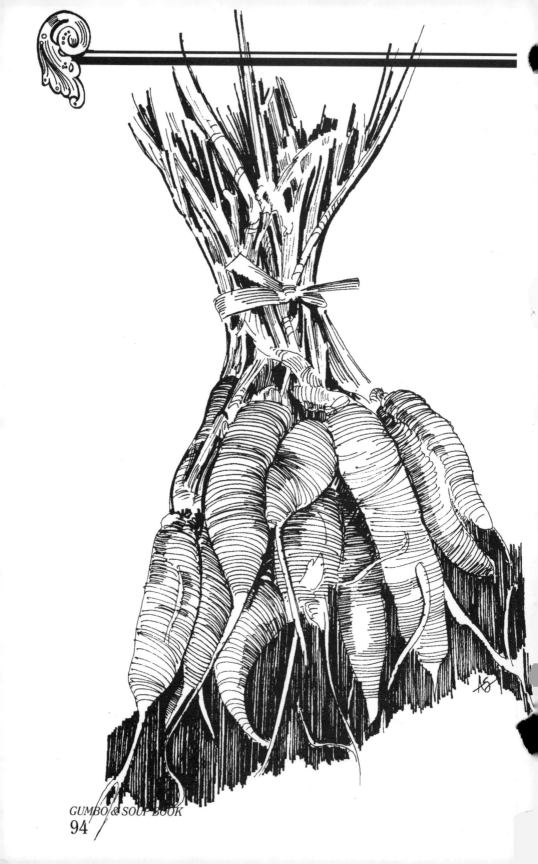